M'Lady's
Book of
Household Secrets

*For Ian, my darling
and loving husband*

M'Lady's Book of Household Secrets

RECIPES, REMEDIES & ESSENTIAL ETIQUETTE

THE HON. SARAH MACPHERSON

The History Press

DISCLAIMER

Always consult your doctor before taking any medication.
Please be advised that this book is a work of historical interest
and the Publishers accept no liability for the efficacy or side-
effects of any of the treatments described.

First published 2013
This paperback edition first published 2023

The History Press
97 St George's Place, Cheltenham,
Gloucestershire, GL50 3QB
www.thehistorypress.co.uk

British Library Cataloguing in Publication Data.
A catalogue record for this book is available from the British Library.

ISBN 978 1 80399 539 7

Typesetting and origination by The History Press
Printed and bound in Great Britain by TJ Books Limited, Padstow, Cornwall

Trees for Life

Contents

Acknowledgements

I would like to thank the following:

Mally Francis, Botanical Illustrator
Charles Francis, Photographer
Katherine Manning, House Steward, Lacock Abbey
Elizabeth Gibb, Meg Holbrook & Marlene Lewis, compilers, Lacock Abbey papers
David Formby, National Trust
Weddingtoncastle.co.uk
Orion Publishing Group
S.P.C.K. Publishing
Michael Slavin, Old Bookshop, Tara
Sir George & Mrs Carmel Locke
Anna Blundell Williams
Diana Turner
Shirley Smith
Katherine Bolder, Design
Ronan Colgan, The History Press
Beth Amphlett, & all the Design Team at The History Press
Ian Macpherson, Editor

Introduction

Eighteenth-century ladies of high society and aristocratic lineage kept handwritten notes on recipes, remedies, gardening and household tips in their personal Household Books. Indeed, it became quite the fashion to exchange their most successful tips with their hosts, as they travelled around staying in some of the grandest houses in the land.

Very few of these fragile House Books have survived. This book celebrates the recent discovery of two new sources: one from Lady Talbot of Lacock Abbey and the other from Lady Louisa Conolly of Castletown.* Both are gems of eighteenth-century history. Also included here are extracts from another eighteenth/nineteenth-century source that describes the life and duties of servants in Weddington Castle.

Gascoine Powder

Take crabs of the sea gathered at constellation time when the sun and moon are in conjuncion in the sign Cancer. They must be alive and dead in that time. Take the shells of the black tips of the claws and beat them to a fine powder in a large brass mortar then sift them through a Tiffiny sieve. The powder must be so fine that it will melt in yr mouth and to 4 ounces of this powder you must add half an ounce of currel finely prepared and so mingle them well together.

Then take a quart of water and put in it vipers' skins cut in pieces about an inch long. Put to them an ounce of leafe gold broake very small. Boyle not dry. When it is cold and strain'd then mingle it with a little rose water wherein a little saffron and 2 grains of Ambergrease have been steep'd. Then make up the powder with the liquor into balls being first finely ground upon a painter's stone.

Addressed to 'My honoured nephew, Sir John Talbot'

These sources transport us into a world of scents and aromas, herbs, oils and tinctures used in every aspect of daily life.

<hr>

'The Heady smell of Pine & Rosemary burning
in the Hearth in the Castle Hall.'

<hr>

These secret remedies and concoctions were used for refreshing the air, the drapes and the carpets, home medicine, cooking, cosmetics and to keep the eighteenth-century garden pest-free.

* See Main Reference and Historical Sources on page 137.

one

Herbal Remedies

During the eighteenth and nineteenth centuries many advances were being made in medical science into the causes of illnesses and the means to help alleviate them. But, despite these advances, many diseases, such as Smallpox, Consumption (Tuberculosis) and Cholera were still endemic (the introduction of Edward Jenner's vaccination in 1798 made Smallpox preventable but many people could not afford it). Convulsions and fits were also commonplace and medical provision by the parish was often basic.

The Wiltshire parish of Laycock, for example, recorded their provision for the sick in 1724, when neighbours were paid to nurse the infirm in their own homes (a matter that caused the parish considerable worry regarding the expense). It wasn't until forty years later that a parish institution was opened in which to house and care for these patients.

For those who could afford it, doctors and apothecaries offered their services, but they were expensive: medical services were performed by contract from 1751 for the sum of ten guineas.

With so many serious illnesses and the expensive nature of what limited professional medical treatment there was available, most people stuck to their old remedies. Many country houses noted these down in their Household Books, some of which still survive to this day.

Here we see the emphasis on herbs, spices, and some quite bizarre ingredients. Garden snails figure in several remedies, either to be taken internally, or as a facewash. Worms, moles and viper skins are more rare ingredients, and a Gascoine Powder contained powdered pearl, gold leaf, and ambergris.

Some remedies are a mixture of knowledge, folklore, and a large measure of desperation.

Herbal Remedies

PREPARING REMEDIES

How to Make a Herbal Infusion

¾ oz of dried herb or 1 oz of fresh herb (use both leaves and flowers)
17 fl oz of freshly boiled water

Steep the herb in a warmed teapot with a lid (this releases the active ingredients) for at least 5 minutes.

Strain into a cup to drink immediately. This infusion can also be cooled in the teapot and strained off into a jar with a tight lid. Store in a cool larder. This can be re-heated and re-used within 24 hours. Drink 1 cup of infusion 3–4 times a day.

Nettle or ginseng infusions can be used as a tonic while chamomile and mint infusions are used for soothing the temperament and can be given all year round. With a good diet and bracing walks, these will give energy, and encourage better sleep.

A sage infusion is good for sore throats (3 leaves infused into a cup of boiled water for 3 minutes) and a peppermint, yarrow and elderflower infusion, taken at bedtime, will keep a cold at bay if given early enough.

⊰ *WARNING* ⊱

Do not use any sage remedies if M'Lady is pregnant,
or breast-feeding a child.

How to Make a Tincture

Mix the herb material with the liquid to a ratio between
1:3 to 1:5. The liquid should be made of water and
alcohol to a ratio of 2:3 to 1:1 (depending on the herb
used). Sugar Beet can be used as the alcohol source. Dilute
the required dose of tincture in hot water before taking.
(Most of the alcohol will evaporate.)

How to Make Concentrated Oils for Healing, Energy and Scent

The oils are extracted from: flowers, leaves, fruit, peel,
seeds, wood, bark, and roots.

It takes 2,000 roses to make one 10ml bottle of rose water so only a tiny amount is needed when it is mixed with creams or lotions – 10–20 drops only in 100ml. This absorbs well into the skin.

NATURE'S INGREDIENTS

Herbal Resins

Benzoin: aromatic resin from Styrax tree. Used as preservative and for healing, it also treats coughs and calms the system.

Myrrh: gum resin from Arab lands. Used against body fungus and for healing.

Powders

Slippery elm: the powdered bark of elm tree. It strengthens, heals, and is used in warm poultices to draw out a foreign body.

Borax: a mineral that has cleaning properties and also acts as an emulsifier in M'Lady's face cream to bind the oils and water together. Only to be used in very small amounts.

⊰ *WARNING* ⊱

Borax is toxic if taken in large amounts.

Spices

Cayenne: Stimulates circulation and increases blood flow.

⊰ *WARNING* ⊱

Cayenne is harmful in big doses.

Cinnamon: Healing, anti-fungus, and good for digestion.

Cloves: Stimulating and warming. They also promote healing, and have a useful pain-masking action.

Ginger: Stimulates circulation and has many uses in home remedies.

⊰ *WARNING* ⊱

High doses of ginger can be toxic.
Do not use when M'Lady is with child.

Nutmeg: Aids digestion, and helps prevent nausea. Carry a whole nutmeg in your pocket to ward off pains in the hips and back. The oil of nutmeg is used in remedies for stiff and aching joints.

⊰ *WARNING* ⊱

Nutmeg can be harmful in large doses.

Herbs in the Bath
Stimulating: basil, bay, fennel, lavender, lemon verbena, lovage, meadowsweet, mint, pine, rosemary, sage, thyme.

Relaxing: catnep, chamomile, jasmine, lime flowers, vervain.

Healing: comfrey, lady's mantle, marigold, mint, yarrow.

Oils and Waxes
Beeswax: an emulsifier for creams and lotions.

Cocoa Butter: a richly moisturising fat.

Coconut Oil: extracted from the white flesh of a coconut, it is an excellent moisturiser for problem skin. This is solid at room temperature but it melts when lukewarm.

COLDS, COUGHS, AND FLU

Magic Cold Remedy

2 cloves garlic
1 teaspoon grated ginger root
2 lemons
1 cup water
2 teaspoons honey
1 cinnamon stick

Crush the garlic, grate the ginger and squeeze the lemons. Boil them in water and pour into a cup. Add garlic, ginger, lemon juice, honey, and cinnamon stick. Leave to cool for 2 minutes. Remove the cinnamon stick and drink while still hot.

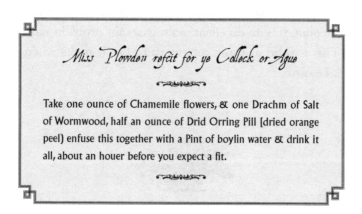

Miss Plowden refcit for ye Colleck or Ague

Take one ounce of Chamemile flowers, & one Drachm of Salt of Wormwood, half an ounce of Drid Orring Pill [dried orange peel] enfuse this together with a Pint of boylin water & drink it all, about an houer before you expect a fit.

Dandelion Cough Syrup

8 oz honey
25 dandelion flower-heads

Put dandelion flower-heads into a pan and add the honey. Pour in enough cold water to cover by at least ¾ inch. Bring to the boil before lowering the heat to simmer while stirring. As the mixture begins to stiffen remove the pan from the heat and pour the mixture through a sieve. Leave to cool and then pour the mixture into well-sterilised jars and seal tightly.

Honey, Lemon and Ginger Drink – for the throat

Juice of 4 lemons
1½ tablespoons honey
1 teaspoon grated ginger root

Pour squeezed lemon juice into small pan over a medium heat. Add the honey and stir. Add the ginger and stir again. Pour into a cup and sip while still hot. To be made fresh and taken twice a day.

For Hiccups

Chervil seeds stirred into vinegar.

Surfit Water

[Probably 'surfeit', although this seems a very rich mixture to cure an excess of eating or drinking]

Take a gallon of Brandy and a peck of Poppys, let them steep together three days. Stirring night and morning, keep them close cover'd then streyn ye Poppys from ye Bran and put into it a half a pd of raisons of ye sun stoned and of figs two oz of liquorish, 2oz of Dates, 2oz of Anefeeds Mint & Balm watter, half a pint of each . Let all these steep togeather close cover'd five or 6 days, stirring twice a day ,then strayn it off for use.

The Recr says you may have a ufefull water by diftilling ye ingredients adding to them some good herbs, half an oz of Mace and ½oz of Nutmeg, a qtr of an oz of Cloves bruifed & some corriander seed.

INSOMNIA AND NERVOUS TENSION

For Interrupted Sleep
Valerian root: take as an infusion.

⊰ *WARNING* ⊱
Do not take valerian root with other herbs.

Lavender: dried lavender flower infusion.

Chamomile: dried infusion helps relaxation.

Basil: take in food or as an infusion. Has a calming effect on the nerves.

Bath-time Relaxation
1 oz hops
1 oz rosemary

Place the hops and rosemary together into a muslin bag and sew it up. Place the bag in a hot bath for 5 minutes before M'Lady gets in. (Chamomile and lavender can also be used with the same method.)

Lavender Nightcap

4 fl oz water

3 tablespoons fresh lavender leaves

1 tablespoon honey

3 tablespoons orange flower water (made with infused orange flowers boiled down to concentrate and stored in a jar with a tight lid)

Put the water, lavender leaves and honey in a pan and place on a gentle heat until the honey dissolves. Strain and add orange flower water. Drink while still warm.

FOR THE WHOLE BODY

To Prevent Infection from Smallpox and other Fevers

One handful of rosemary

One handful of rue sage

One handful of lavender

One handful of wormwood

One handful of mint

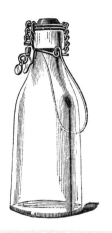

Strip the herb leaves from their stalks, and chop them very small. Put them into a stone jar with one pint of the very best white wine vinegar. Stop with a well-fitted stopper and let it stand before the fire for 3–4 days. Strain off the liquor and pour

Miss Plowden Recept for ye Dropsie

Take ye branch leaves of Artichoques, & pound in a Morter & strain 'm & put ye liquer into a bottle & keep it till you have a fit of the Dropsie, then take a spoonful or more of that liquor at a time, & put it into a glass of white wine & drink it twice a day, morning & afternoon. It will purge you by urine, but if that quantity does not doe it enough, you may repeat it as you see occasion.

what is clear liquid into a bottle with 1 oz of camphire. Keep the bottle closed and shake it well before use.

When M'Lady first goes into the air of any infected place, rub her lips and nostril with the infusion.

To Overcome Shyness
Make a thyme and beer soup using a chicken stock base.

To Remove Inhibitions and to use as an Aphrodisiac
Concentrated oil of ylang ylang.

For a Bileous Complaint

A quarter of a Pound of Dandelion with its Roots clean'd and cut small and half an ounce of currants bruised. Boil them gently in a Pint of water till half the Liquid is wasted, then strain it off and preſs out as much of the juice as you can – add it to half an ounce of Tincure of Senna and half a Dram of Tincure of Cardamums.

Take half at going to Bed, and the other half in the Morning.

This medicine should be repeated ev'ry Night & Day for a fortnight & then twice a week and then once a week. It succeeds best when the Stomach is empty and no Supper is eat – and then the stomach is often relieved by drinking the Tea made of Dandelion alone cut small.

Use when in an Expectant State

Concentrated mandarin oil is safe to use on a kerchief. (It is also good for calming children.)

To Clean-Out the System – A Two-Day Regime

To be used 2/3 times a year. All drinks use cooled boiled water.

Day 1: 1 glass of cooled boiled water with juice of ½ a lemon in the morning

Eat grapes whenever hungry (3lbs + during the day)

You should drink at least 10 glasses of liquid a day, of which one half can be diluted juices (carrot, celery or apple juice taken with 50 per cent water) and the other half water, or teas (peppermint, chamomile or ginger)

Day 2: Mixed vegetable soup made with artichoke, beetroot, broccoli, cabbage, carrots, celery, lettuce, onion, and watercress.

Miss Plowden Sis: Bell Day,
Recept for ye Yallow or Black Janders [Jaundice]

Take fanerick, tumeryrick & inward Bard of Barbary dryed to a powder, sift them threw a sieve & 2 peny-worth, ground small. Devide it in 3 parts, & take for three Mornings, as much of each as will lye on a sixpence, in a draft of white Wine, warmed with a gad of steel. Fast for a time after you drink it. Repeat as oft as you have occasion.

An Alternative Quick Cleansing of the System (also for the skin)

Give a thistle and milk hot drink at bedtime.

Against Body Odour

Apple cider vinegar
Water
Ammonium Alum
Castor-oil plant extract

Mix equal parts of apple cider vinegar and water. Pat it onto the underarms. Leave the arms outstretched, and wait until it has dried before adding ammonium alum and castor-oil plant extract.

Please note: with this treatment, the patient can still perspire. Eating red meat is the main cause of body odour so reducing consumption can also help.

Lovage crunch up into a muslin sachet and placed in the bath can also be used to mask body odours.

For Monthly Problems and Bloating
A warm nettle tea infusion will calm the pains, and reduce the bloating.

To Cheer up the Moods, Stimulate the Liver and for Fluid Retention
A vitality salad of the following leaves: dandelion, baby spinach, arigula (rocket), lamb's lettuce, spearmint, a few lemon balm leaves, borage flowers, pot marigold petals, with a lemon & oil dressing.

For Worms

Of Myrrh, Aloes and Mitheradate, each a gr of an once, a little powder of dry'd wormwood. Mix these into a paste with frexh Ox of Bulls Gall & spread it upon sheeps leather. Lay it upon the person's stomach with the point upwards and the bottom not to touch the navel by 2 fingers breadth. When it has lain on 24 hours let the person take gentle Physick every other day for three times and about 10 days after a dose rather stronger. Let the plaister lye on as long as will stick. If it makes the stomach itch and break out into little spots, lay the skin of mutton suet on when you take the plaister off. The above quantity of ingredients will spread a great many Plaisters but it must not be mixed with Gall until you use it. If the person is too weak to take the Physick let them have the following Glister as you judge proper for three or four times.

The Glister

Of wormwood and wormseed of each half an ounce (this is enough for 3 Glisters). Boil it in thin gruel or small broath. When enough put in a spoonful of coarse sugar and strain it. Give a young child half a pint – more in proportion to age. The person or child must not eat milk or fruit so long as the Plaister lyes on. It will not stick if the person has not worms.

[This is followed by a diagram of the shape of the plaster. Mitheradat is a composite medicine used as a panacea. 'Glister' is an enema, see plate section]

To Fight off Illness, Infections and Depression

6–8 nasturtium leaves and flowers
Bunch watercress (stalks off)
1 oz chopped parsley
Lettuce leaves
Thin peeled cucumber slice
1 large peeled and quartered orange

Mix together to form a nasturtium and watercress salad.

½ teaspoon garlic pulp with a little salt rubbed in
1 teaspoon light mustard
3 teaspoons saffron flower oil
1 teaspoon orange flower water
1 teaspoon lemon juice
Small bunch of finely chopped chives
Pinch of ground black pepper

Put all the dressing ingredients into a tight jar and shake well. Drizzle the dressing over the salad and use the reserved nasturtium flowers for decoration.

Lady Northumberland's Worm Broth for a Consumption

Take a knuckle of veal & the neck end of mutton, an ounce of French Barley wch must be boyled first in water & let yr meat boyle first then put to it pennyroyal hearts tongues leaves, liverwort marygold flowers a little maiden hair & some other cooling herbs according to yr discression.

Then take 50 angle worms, cut off their heads and tails, thrust a bodkin through 'em to slit 'em, then scower them with salt & wash 'em in several waters till they are very clean. Put them in after the meat is boyled and skim'd & let em boyle together from 7 o'clock in the morning till ten at night & it will be strong broth but do not let it boyle too fast. Strain and drink of it morning and evening warm but never skim it after the worms are put in.

For the Ricketts or Weakness in the Joints

Take of May Butter fresh from the butter milk one pound and a pound of sheep's suet where in the kidney was enclosed. As many wild white Primrose Leaves as one can hold between both our Hands. The same quantity of Long planton leaves. The same of Green tops of Elder. The same of Malows if you have Marsh Mallows else the common sort will do.

A pint of Large Shell Snails. Shred the Herbs & Suet & pound it all in a mortar then stew it over the fire. When it is well stewed the ointment looks green, strain through a linnen cloth, for use (it may be set in a pot in the oven to stew). When it is cold if there is some drops in the bottom you may melt it again & powder it off to keep for use.

HANDS

Gentle Sugar Scrub Massage

2 tablespoons rich oil (olive etc.)
3 tablespoons sugar

Mix to a paste. Rub hands with a small amount, and massage it in gently for 1 minute. Rinse well with warm water and dry well. To be used at least once a week.

Skin Care for Dry Hands

1 tablespoon honey
2 tablespoon softened butter

Mix the honey and butter together. Apply to clean hands and massage in well for 2 minutes then wipe off with a hand cloth.

Potato Hand Mask

Mash potato with milk till it resembles thick cream. Massage into the hands and leave on for 2–3 minutes. Rinse and dry the hands.

To Soften the Hands

1 tablespoon of vinegar
200 ml water

Wash hand regularly with the solution.

SKIN CARE

Sprouting Seeds for Acne

Most seed can be sprouted, for example: wheat, maize, coriander, sunflower, radish, clover, and broccoli seeds (but not oats).

3 tablespoons of seed
Cold water

Use a flat-bottomed container with a neck. Add 3 tablespoons of seeds and half fill the container with cold water. Stretch some muslin over the neck and secure with a tie and leave to soak overnight. Pour water away by straining it through the muslin cover and place the bottle in warm natural sunlight (but not direct sunlight). Twice a day, rinse the seeds in cold water, draining well each time. Turn the container regularly to ensure the sun gets to all sides.

The seeds will be ready to eat after 4–5 days. Eat immediately.

Acne Masks
Honey
Cinnamon powder

Make a paste of honey and cinnamon powder. Apply it just before bedtime. Wash off with warm water in the morning.

Alternative Acne Treatments
Rub fresh garlic on and around pimples and leave on for as long as possible.

Both lavender oil and mandarin oil can be applied undiluted to small areas of skin. It can be dabbed straight onto pimples and reduces the inflammation. (Mandarin oil is especially good for blackheads).

For Pimples and Scaly Skin
Raw carrot juice, taken twice a day.

For Dry Wrinkly Skin
20 poppy petals
10 fl oz boiling water

Put the poppy petals into the boiling water and leave to infuse for 10 minutes. Strain,

and allow to cool before bottling it securely. Use last thing at night and first in the morning.

Nettle tea makes the skin more supple.

Rose hip oil is ideal for dry, mature, and sensitive skins. It also heals cuts, treats scars, and reduces wrinkles.

A diet should especially include: apples, cranberries, celery, berry-fruits, onions, kale, parsley, beetroot, and tomatoes.

Mature Complexions

Extract the steam distillation of the resin in the Myrrh Bush. This is soothing for mature skin. It also heals infected, cracked or chapped skin.

For Oily Skin

Lightly dab rose water on M'Lady's skin before applying the greases, powders and rouges. Never use hot water on oily skin.

Pineapple Cleanser

Cut a thin slice of raw pineapple, and gently run it over the face (but not around the eyes). This lifts dead cells. Leave it on for five minutes and gently wash it off with just-warm water.

Buttermilk Cleanser

5 fl oz buttermilk
2 tablespoons elder flowers

Heat the buttermilk, add the flowers and boil gently for half an hour. Remove from heat and leave to infuse for 2 hours. Strain. Apply with gentle round motions. This removes all dirt and face-powder. Gentle but effective.

Face Toner

Apple Cider Vinegar
Oil (lavender, rose, or rosemary)
Cold water

Put 1–2 tablespoons of vinegar into 8 fl oz water. Add up to 5 drops of oil, and blend.

For Skin Tone and Thread Veins

Oil of Neroli, distilled from flowers of the bitter orange tree. It is good for all skin types and ages, but best for mature skin, inflammation, irritation or redness. It tones

the complexion and reduces thread vein. It also calms the mental state as its sweet floral aroma creates the feeling of euphoria.

For Eczema, Dermatitis, and Psoriasis

Chamomile extraction. It is calming and soothing and can be used for redness or inflamed conditions, spots, and acne. It has an especial ability to heal wounds without scarring.

Rosemary extraction can also be used for dermatitis and psoriasis and also gets rid of headaches, greasy hair, scalp, and dandruff.

For Sunburn

Too much sun on the face is the cause of early skin ageing. A wide-brimmed hat must always be worn and a veil is needed in hot countries.

Run a tepid bath, add a cupful of apple cider vinegar (which calms the hurt), a tablespoon of almond oil (to stop the skin drying out), and fifteen drops of lavender oil (to repair the sun damage). Mix well into the bath water. Red sunburnt skin will turn brown, without peeling.

For smaller areas of sunburn, treat with neat lavender oil.

Aloe Vera is soothing and cooling for larger areas of sunburn. Add a few drops of peppermint oil to produce a cooling effect.

Diet for the Protection from the Sun

Vegetables (eaten raw or steamed): carrots and all dark green vegetables, like spinach, broccoli, green beans, peas, and kale.

Fruit: cherries, blackcurrants, bilberries, and other brightly-coloured edible fruits.

For Bee Stings

Crush the leaves of rue and rub into affected area (but beware the stench). Alternatively costmary (also known as alecost) may be used (this is more usually used to flavour ale).

M'Lady's Full Body Skin-Brushing Regime

Dry the body vigorously all over and brush the skin with a dry softish brush for 2–3 minutes. Start at the feet with small circular strokes. Brush up the legs in long rounded strokes (be sure not to make the skin too red). Brush from the fingertips to the shoulder and towards the Heart using smaller strokes, with the edge of the brush for slightly more pressure. The abdomen to be brushed with circular clock-wise motion only. Avoid the face and any sensitive areas. Keep the brush for this use only. Wash it in water and dry before re-use. M'Lady must be kept relaxed during this brushing, or the skin will not be supple. This removes dead skin cells, tightens the skin and improves digestion. To be performed once a week before taking a bath.

THE EYES

Tea Pads
Cut small muslin pads and soak them in a cold tea solution. Squeeze out the excess liquid, and lay them gently on closed eyelids. Leave for 10 minutes. (Can also be used for tired feet or mild sunburn.)

Tea Bags
Place 1 teaspoon of tea into two small soft bags, and sew them up. Soak the bags in a little hot water, cool till tepid, and place over closed eyes for 10–15 minutes.

Potato Soothers
Cut two halves of a round slice of raw potato. Place one under each eye and leave for 20 minutes.

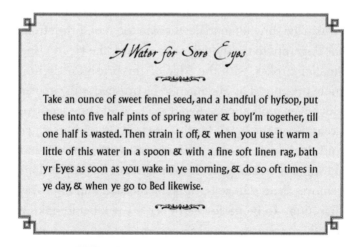

A Water for Sore Eyes

Take an ounce of sweet fennel seed, and a handful of hyfsop, put these into five half pints of spring water & boyl'm together, till one half is wasted. Then strain it off, & when you use it warm a little of this water in a spoon & with a fine soft linen rag, bath yr Eyes as soon as you wake in ye morning, & do so oft times in ye day, & when ye go to Bed likewise.

The Rume Plaister

Take two pennyworth of soft Bruegaldary pitch, one pennorth of venes turpentine, as much pure Ronsen as the end of your thum, as much stone pitch as your fist. Melt all these together in an Earthen Cuppe, & keep it for use. You must apply this plaisters on boath your temples & it will stop the rume from falling down into yr Eyes. It must be scraped very fine, & spred upon black Velvit with a hot knife, & put as hot upon the temples as you can endure it.

For Puffy Eyes

Mash together strawberry and cucumber. Apply under both eyes, and leave for 15–20 minutes.

For Puffy or Strained Eyes

Dip small soft muslin bags into cold milk, or rose water. Lie down with the feet higher than the body. Place the bags on closed eyes and relax for 10 minutes.

☞ Important Pressure Point

Press the mound on the palm of the hand, just below the index finger. Highly recommended for strained and puffy eyes.

FACE MASKS

(The old Roman recipe used raw eggs with honey.)

Forehead and Nose only (all skin types)

2 tablespoons rosewater
1 tablespoon curd
1 tablespoon honey

Mix ingredients together and rub onto skin. Leave for 8–10 minutes, and wash off with hand-warm water.

Avacado Mask

Mash the inside of half an avocado until creamy. Massage into the face and neck and leave for 15–20 minutes. Gently wash off with warm water, and dab the skin lightly with cold tea.

For Drier and More Mature Skin
(A Most Favourite Mask)

Add a little honey to the mashed Avacado Mask (above).

Egg White Mask

Cover the face with raw egg, having first removed the yoke. Allow to dry and wash off with warm water after 10 minutes.

For Oily Skin

Add 1 teaspoon lemon juice and 1 teaspoon honey to the Avacado Mask (above).

Alternative Mask for Oily Skin

Half a small banana
1 teaspoon hemp oil
1 teaspoon honey

Mash the ingredients together, apply to the skin and leave for 10 minutes. Gently wash off with warm water.

For Extra Oily Skin

Add 1 tablespoon fine oatmeal to the Banana Mask (above).

HAIR

Society ladies of the eighteenth century wore the latest fashion: 'high hair', said to have been introduced by the fun-loving Duchess of Devonshire. Lady Louisa Conolly from Castletown wrote to her sisters, laughing at herself, of having to sit upon the floor of her carriage – or she would not fit in.

Hair powders were in vogue, and sometimes took hours to apply. Lady Louisa's Lady's Maid prepared the herbal powders herself, which included arris root and rosemary leaf to give it the holding lift. The whole structure was concocted around a tall mesh dome-shape attached to the skull. If they were not properly fixed the 'high hair' would collapse sideways.

Oils for Different Hair Types

Normal: eucalyptus, cedarwood, geranium, orange, lavender

Oily: basil, bergamot, cypress, grapefruit, lavender, lemon

Dry: frankincense, palmarosa, sandalwood, rosemary

Damaged: comfrey, horsetail, frankincense

Fine: geranium

Dark: rosemary, thyme

Fair: chamomile

Frequent Wash: geranium, horsetail, lavender, rosemary

Thinning Hair: basil, sage, cypress, palmarosa, rosemary, thyme, cedarwood

Dandruff: cedarwood, rosemary, sage, tea-tree, thyme, patchouli

For Dark Hair and Flaky Itchy Skin
Rinse hair with diluted cider vinegar, 1 tablespoon vinegar in 8 fl oz water.

For Fair Hair and Greasy Scalp
Rinse with diluted juice of half a lemon in 8 fl oz water.

⊰ *WARNING* ⊱
Never rub the hair dry – Pat it dry. (Hair splits if it is rubbed)

Scalp Massage for Itchy Flaky Skin
Almond, avocado and olive oils.

For Sleekness and Volume (Dark Hair)
Rub brown ale into the hair and roots (black porter is too sticky).

FOR THE OLFACTORY SENSES (THE NOSE)

Pot-Pourri
1 cup of heavily-scented rose petals
1 cup of lavender flowers
6 crushed bay-leaves
1 cup each of lemon verbena, marjoram, and thyme
1 tablespoon of orris root powder
1 teaspoon allspice
A few dried, crushed cloves

All ingredients must already be dried before mixing together.

Tussie-Mussie (Pomander)
2 tablespoons dried lavender flowers
1 tablespoon sweet flag root powder
1 tablespoon ground gum benzoin
2 teaspoons sandalwood powder
6 drops of lavender essence

3 drops of ambergris
1 teaspoon powdered gum tragacanth
8 teaspoons orange-flower water
Lavender oil

Grind the dried lavender flowers to fine powder. Sift into a bowl with sweet flag, gum benzoin, and sandalwood powders. Mix well and add essence of lavender and ambergris. Make a paste by mixing the tragacanth with the orange-flower water, then roll all the other ingredients into the paste. Rub your hands in a little lavender oil, and break the paste into small equal pieces. Roll each one into a round shape. and make a hole through the middle with a large needle. Leave to dry in a dark drawer for a week and then string them for use. [Travellers carried these on the road to keep bad odours and infections away.]

Herb Pillow

9 inch square muslin, stuffed with lavender, lemon, verbena, or sweet woodruff, and sewn up. Cover the muslin with another 9 inch square cotton outer layer, with soft wadding in the edges and sew together. Slip it under M'Lady's normal pillow for a scented sleep.

LIPS

The lips are more attractive to a man just before the monthly. Beeswax protects the lips. Young ladies must avoid licking or biting their lips.

For Sore Lips

Treat with honey and a little olive oil.

NAILS AND TEETH

Toothpowder

4 teaspoons sage leaf
3 teaspoons salt
1 teaspoon myrrh

Mix all the together. Place the mixture on an open tray and heat in oven for 30 minutes (med. temp.). Remove from heat and allow to cool for 10 minutes, then grind finely with a pestle and mortar. Press the mixture through a fine sieve and throw away any lumps. Use with a mouth brush. It dissolves in the mouth and is gently abrasive and acts against infection.

Alternative Toothpowder

Pick wild wet seaweed. Wash the sand off it gently with a little cold water. Make an infusion of roots, stems, and leaves. Apply at bedtime and wash off in the morning.

FEET

Exercise for the Feet

Place 10 marbles (or other small round stones) on floor. With bare feet pick them up one by one with the toes and place them into a wide bowl.

Soothing Massage for the Feet

Using the same marbles (or stones), place a layer of marbles in the bottom of a large foot bowl (so they cover ¾ of the base). Add enough warm water to cover the feet and add half a cup of salt, and 3 drops of scented oil. Place the feet in the bowl and gently glide the feet along the marbles for a soothing massage for 10 minutes.

For Cold Feet

Add 1–2 teaspoons of freshly shredded ginger to a bowl of warm water, and soak feet for 10–20 minutes. Rinse and dry.

Alternatively put 2 tablespoons of powdered mustard dissolved in a foot bowl of hot water. Soak the feet for 15–20 minutes. Rinse and dry.

ANTI-AGEING EXERCISES
(FROM LADY TALBOT'S LADY'S MAID)

Neck and Throat

Sit upright, tilt head back and look at ceiling. With lips closed, make chewing movement. This works the muscles in throat and neck to excellent effect. Repeat 20 times.

Still looking at ceiling, close and relax the lips. Pucker them into a kiss-shape, and then stretch the kiss outwards – extending the lips. Keep the lips puckered for a count of 10. Then relax to normal position. Repeat 20 times.

Cheeks

Have a relaxed smile, with lips closed. Suck in the cheeks to touch the teeth and hold for a count of 20. Relax and repeat 20 times.

Sit in front of a mirror. Smile as broadly as possible with lips closed, and with mouth corners turned up. Try to make mouth corners touch the ears! Wrinkle up the nose and see the cheeks muscles move upwards. Stay like that for a count of 20. Repeat 20 times.

⊰ *WARNING* ⊱

There may be minor blemishes after the first time these exercises for the face and neck are completed. Your Lady's skin will get used to the exercises, and will look much better after the third or fourth time.

Eyes

Place 2 fingers on each side of the head at temples, and press while opening and closing the eyes rapidly. Repeat 20 times.

Small lines at the sides of the eyes and puffiness can be reduced by eye-tapping. Tap gently with the pads of the fingers from the inside corner (near the nose) to the outer edge, and back again (following the curve under the eye). Repeat 20 times.

Forehead

Frown as much as possible. Try to bring the eyebrows over the eyes, while also pulling them towards one another. Then lift the eyebrows as high as possible, while opening the eyes as wide as possible. Repeat 20 times.

Lips

Sit upright facing forward. Keep lips closed and teeth together smile as broadly as possible (without opening the lips). Keep like this for a count of 20 and relax. Then pucker the lips into a pointed kiss and keep this for a count of 20 and relax. Repeat 20 times.

Sleeping Positions

Ladies will see deep lines appear on their cheeks and chin over time if they sleep on their side, with their faces crushed against the pillow. They must try to sleep on their back so that these wrinkles will not develop.

⊰ *WARNING* ⊱

Crying into a pillow causes salt deposits to dry
in the wrinkles and will accelerate ageing.
Cheer her up!

two

Household Maintenance

CLEANING

Nature's Deterrents

Wormwood: use as a fly deterrent when sprays are hung up in room and as a moth deterrent if hung in M'Lady's wardrobe.

Lad's Love: also a moth deterrent amongst the clothes.

Curry Plant: a pungent moth deterrent.

Woodruff: pick at flowering time. When dried it smells of new-mown hay. Strew it onto floors. smelling sweetly.

Pennyroyal: very strong odour of peppermint. Crush the leaves and place them in beds against fleas. (Keep a lot of this to hand near the Linen Room.)

Lavender: for the scenting of drawers and wardrobes. Pick the lavender just before the heads open. Dry them and pull off the stems. Prepare $2\frac{1}{2}$in square cotton pieces. Fill the squares with the lavender heads and sew up.

Nature's Cleansers

Bicarbonate of Soda: de-odorises, absorbent and gently abrasive. Cleans hard surfaces, crayons and ink. Mix with water to make a paste to polish silver.

Lemon: high acid makes it an excellent grease cutter and stain remover. Good bleaching ability. Removes limescale from taps and rust marks, as well as fruit-based stains from white fabric. Removes tarnish from brass and copper and disinfects larder and kitchen tiles.

Salt: shifts stubborn stains on hard surfaces, removes baked-on food on kitchen dishes and unblocks drains.

⊰ *WARNING* ⊱

Do not put salt into metal and do not use it on a carpet.

Soapwort (or latherwort): was invaluable in old houses. It was used to clean and restore the colours of delicate fabrics like tapestries and brocade curtains.

Vinegar: Cuts grease, dissolves scum, shines windows and glass (use 1 part vinegar to 4 parts water). A half cupful is used in the last rinse of clothes.

Rhubarb and sorrel: used in kitchens, boiled in water, to clean the pans.

A-Z of Cleaning

Alabaster: looks like marble and is used for statues, ornaments and portrait plaques. It is softer than marble and can easily be chipped or bruised. It is not to be washed in plain water (it dissolves). Clean with softest brush and lightly polish with wax if wanted (but take care not to discolour). If the alabaster is very marked a soft flannel dipped in a little turpentine, and then in powered pumice, may be used. Then wash in a little borax with warm soapy water, and dry and polish with a soft rag.

Amber: if rubbed with a woollen cloth it creates static and attracts fluff, scraps of paper, and dust. Rubbing with a dry soft cotton cloth releases a pleasant odour of pine forests and musk. Never wash amber with water as it will become opaque. Remove dirt by gently rubbing with French chalk on a soft cotton cloth.

Arms and armour: wear cotton gloves to clean or you will leave finger-marks behind. Carefully remove swords from their sheaths. (You may have to use light vegetable oil to free it, if it is stuck in its scabbard. Leave oil on for 2 days, and gently tap on the hilt of the sword to release it.) Use the finest scrubbing wool soaked in light oil and soap. Bad rust can be loosened very carefully with oil on the finger then rubbed very gently with scrubbing wool. Some handles and hilts may be surrounded in leather. These will have to be re-covered. To re-cover: Soak a thin piece of leather of the right size in water to make it supple, ease it into place over the metal or wood base, and sew along the edges with strong matching threads. (While still damp, you can emboss or work a pattern into it.) Lastly, colour it with natural dyes to match if needed.

Baize: generally used as a noise and smell guard, green baize is used for games tables, screens, for protection for the bottom of tea caddies, and for covering doors between the kitchen quarters and the formal reception rooms.

A double door with baize is also used to soundproof the schoolroom area. Liquid spills must be treated immediately with a clean linen cloth before it dries on. Some dry stains may be removed by dabbing with a cloth damped in soapy water and rubbing very gently – but do not rub too hard.

Bamboo furniture: clean bamboo by scrubbing with warm soapy water and a strong brush. Dry carefully and treat with honey wax.

Barometers: leave well alone!

Books: never bang a book to dust it; using a soft shaving brush, hold the book along the front edge, dust downwards, away from the spine, taking care of the corners and edges of the binding at the back. Damaged and dry leather spines will respond to careful massaging with a soft non-scented soap on a damp finger. If there is damp in the pages, open the book, and stand it on one end with the leaves fanned out. Leave to dry in a warmish place, not with direct heat. Once dry, take the book outdoors and gently brush the

loose mildew deposits off. (Important – find the cause of the damp.)

Bottles: if the bottles are discoloured. Fill with a little water and add tea leaves. Gently drop in a ball-bearing and swirl it round and round.

Bronzes: never clean with abrasives, spirits, or water. Lightly dust with a cotton cloth only, then rub over with a soft cloth dipped in linseed oil.

⊰ *WARNING* ⊱

The use of any salts will corrode a bronze and create permanent green-coloured damage.

Cane work: dirt accumulates in cane chairs, in the mesh of the weaving. Scrub with a stiff brush and warm soapy water. Ingrained grime needs quickly dunking in a bath of warm soapy water, then dabbed with light flour using a small paintbrush. Allow to dry naturally and brush off. Then rinse the cane work in cold water and leave it in an airy place to dry.

Carpets: everyday regime: Fold the carpet back in half, brush floor underneath (and take away the dirt). Brush the two back halves before the front. Never take the edges of a carpet and shake it. Smaller carpets can be draped over a line in good weather. Tap it firmly but gently all over to dislodge the dirt. Never beat a valuable carpet.

A fresh wine stain must be pressed with a clean cloth to soak up as much liquid as possible. Then sprinkle a thick layer of salt onto the stain. Leave this on until it is dry and brush off.

Grease stains will come off with fuller's earth. Dust the powder over the affected area, leave for 24 hours, and brush away. Wax can be removed by placing blotting paper underneath as well as on top of the carpet and ironing the spot with a warm (not too hot) iron. Repeat with more clean blotting paper until the wax is gone.

To restore a faded carpet brush it well and put a tablespoon of salt and ¼ pint of vinegar into a container of hot water, and rub the carpet well with the solution. This restores the colour and removes greasy marks.

Copper: copper utensils must be very thoroughly cleaned to avoid the formation of vertigris, which is poisonous. Wash the copper well in hot water, then with a piece of flannel rub on a mixture of salt, fine sand, and vinegar. Wash the copper again in warm water so all traces of vinegar are removed. Dry and polish. A little oil rubbed over the metal occasionally will keep it bright.

Dolls: their faces and other exposed parts (like hands) have to be treated with great care. Remove surface dirt with cosmetic cleansing cream with a soft cloth.

To clean dolls' hair: First take time to untangle the hair very carefully, starting at the ends. Then apply heated bran to the hair, work it in with your fingertips. Leave for 5 minutes and brush it out.

The original clothes of an old doll should be preserved. Carefully sew any damage as discreetly as possible.

Felt hats: rub bran over the surface of the felt. Be sure to remove the bran completely with a soft brush.

Furniture: mix vinegar and warm water, burnish with a soft leather or a cotton cloth.

Alternative furniture cleaner (good for removing sticky marks): Mix 1 tablespoon of turpentine, 3 tablespoons of linseed oil, and 2 pints of hot water. Stir well and allow to cool. Bottle and keep.

Human spit is one of the most effective cleaning substances and costs nothing. 'Spit and Polish' has few equals in everyday care of antiques. Water is usually least effective. Soft cotton and soft brushes should be used. Keep the brushes washed, clean and dry with soap.

Furs: fuller's earth cleans furs. Sprinkle it on, leave to settle, and shake it out carefully.

Gilt frames: take 1½ pints of water and add enough flowers of sulphur to give the water a golden tinge. In this water boil four or five bruised onions. Strain off the liquid, and when cold, use it to wash any gilding which needs restoring, using a soft brush.

Glass: old hard-water and wine stains need strong treatment. Fill the glass with colourless vinegar. Leave for 24 hours and rinse out. If further treatment is needed use egg shells in water.

Gloves (white kid): if only slightly soiled, rub them with cream of tartar. If very dirty, use a piece of rag dipped in carbon tetrachloride. Allow the rag to almost dry before rubbing it on the gloves. Later, the gloves must be rubbed with breadcrumbs until all the stain is removed.

Guns: light oil is usually enough for cleaning guns. With muzzle loaders, to check it is still not loaded, slide a piece of dowel down the barrel and mark its length – then measure it against the outside of the barrel. If it is still full of charge, take great care in removing the ball, wad, and powder. Use the cleaning rod, and make sure it is screwed into the ball. If it is not possible to get the ball out, the gun must be taken to a gunsmith at once.

To clean the wooden part of a gun: Always clean the

wood in the direction of the grain. First rub with fine scrubbing wool, then clean it with cotton cloth dipped in sugar-based alcohol. (Any dents in wooden parts can be reduced by applying a damp cloth to the area; over 2 to 3 days the wood will swell to help fill the dent.) Finally, polish the wood with boiled linseed oil.

Horn: do not immerse in water. Clean with the softest cloth, damped with warm soapy water. Then rinse with another soft cloth wetted in clean water. Dry well with a third cloth. Do not wet the horn at all if it is painted.

Ivory, bone and antler: antlers attract the dust. They should be wiped with a soft cloth damped in mentholated spirits. Polish with wax polish.

Ivory and bone can crack with changes of temperature. Keep pianos away from heat or direct sunlight. Clean with a soft brush and wipe with a soft cloth damped in warm slightly soapy water. Rinse with a clean cloth and

dry with a third soft, colourless cloth. Do not use water on painted or gilded ivory or bone.

Use almond oil (sparingly) on uncoloured surfaces like piano keys. Paint it on with a fine brush until it all looks oily. Leave for eight hours and wipe away surplus oil with some clean soft cloths.

Jewellery: perfume tarnishes the stones so do not put fragrances where a necklace or earrings touch the skin. The harder the stone, the more it scratches its neighbour in the jewellery box. Wrap up each single item and pin brooches onto velvet and keep in airtight box.

Use warm soapy water in a bowl to wash jewellery, in case a stone comes loose and disappears down the sink. Softer stones like amber, jet, pearls, coral, opal, marcasite and tourmaline – wipe with a warm soft cloth. Or soak your pieces of jewellery separately for a few minutes in a glass of gin (do not leave them overnight like the fashion). Do not wash pearls, the string will rot; rub gently with a warm dry cloth instead. Real pearls can also be cleaned by rubbing with a silk handkerchief.

Lace (silk): soak in hot milk and borax to prevent it turning yellow. Do not store silk lace in white paper. Use blue paper and ensure that it completely covers the lace, leaving none exposed.

Lace (old): steep it in water with borax dissolved in it. Wash it out the next day in soapy water, and rinse several times. Then dip the lace into warm water to which several spoonful's of sugar has been added. Pin the lace out on a cloth to dry.

Very valuable old lace should not use the above method. It should be folded up with dry powdered magnesia sprinkled between each fold, and left for some days to allow the powder to absorb some of the dirt.

Lampshades: old lampshades made of vellum should be kept pliable by rubbing over with a cloth moistened with linseed oil.

Marble: mix equal parts of soft soap, quicklime, and caustic potash. Apply with a brush, and leave on the marble for several days, after which it must be wiped off. The marble can then be polished with a mixture of $\frac{1}{2}$lb of washing soda, $\frac{1}{2}$lb of powdered chalk and $\frac{1}{2}$lb of pumice stone. Sift these through a fine sieve and mix into a paste with water. Rub the paste over the marble, leave for several hours and then wash with soap and water. Then give a final polish.

Mother-of-Pearl: the interior surface of sea shells. To clean breathe on it and then rub it with a finger. It can be wiped with a damp cloth with warm soapy water, but do not allow it to get too wet.

Oil paintings: this is not for very valuable paintings. For minor cleaning: Start in a small area at the side to check the effects. Use a cotton cloth damped with spit. Work in a circular motion, changing the face of the cloth as it becomes dirty. If you find paint as well as dirt on the cloth, stop at once.

Paintings can be freshened-up by rubbing a freshly-cut slice of potato dampened in cold water over the surface. Dry and polish with a silk cloth. The surface should then be rubbed over with a flannel very slightly dampened with linseed oil.

Ostrich feathers: to dry clean and curl an ostrich feather, hold it in sulphur fumes – in the open air. To clean an ostrich feather without curling it: make a soapy lather, dip the feather into it, and squeeze it gently between the fingers to get rid of the dirt. When it is quite clean, it must be rinsed in cold water, and laid flat on a clean towel. The feather must then be dabbed rapidly with a soft handkerchief until the fronds are light and fluffy.

Paper: dust the document with a soft brush to remove all surface dirt. If there is mould – take it and brush it off outdoors. Use a cuttlefish-bone as a gentle abrasive to remove spots.

Piano keys: for yellowish ivory keys apply a mixture of equal parts methylated spirits and water, using a squeezed-out pad of absorbent cotton wool.

Shoes: furniture or floor polish is just as good as 'shoe shine'. To remove stains from brown shoes or boots, cut a piece of lemon and rub it on well, then polish with a banana skin.

Silver: add ½ cup soda crystals to 1 pint water. Rub the silver with this solution and the tarnish will be gone after 10 minutes. You can also use bicarbonate of soda. Old powder-puffs washed and dried give a good finish.

Skin rugs: hot bran is used on the palm of the hands to clean skin rugs, working in a circular motion. Shake the rug well to remove all the bran.

Stone: if the front stone steps or window sills are stained, add a little paraffin to hot soapy water and scrub the marks with this.

Tiles: use the ash from open fires to clean the stains off the tiles.

Vases and decanters: a handful of uncooked rice or crushed egg-shells in a small amount of hot water, swirled around the base will remove port, brandy, and dirty water stains.

Wallpaper: soot marks on wallpaper near a fireplace can easily be removed by rubbing gently with a piece of bread.

To remove grease and grime on a small area it is necessary to be very patient. Heat an iron until hand-hot only. Hold a clean absorbent cloth against the wall and press on the cloth. Eventually the heat loosens the dirt and the cloth absorbs the stain. Alternatively, make a thick paste from cleaning fluid and

French chalk. Apply to the spot, leave overnight, and brush off carefully. Repeat if necessary.

Windows: use plain water with a dash of vinegar in it. Apply with a chamois leather. Old newspapers can be used to give a final polish (wear gloves to prevent the fingers going black with the print).

REPAIRS

For Dents in Carpets Caused by Heavy Chairs and Tables

To get pile up again get a small ice block from the Ice House. Over the dent, dissolve the ice block with hot water. The steam and the ice block contents will raise the carpet pile up again.

For Rotten Furniture Legs

Where wood has rotted so that legs can no longer be held securely. Pick out the area of rotten wood. Pack the enlarged cavity with a hard filler made up of sawdust and animal-glue bound together before replacing the leg.

Mother-of-Pearl

Any missing fragments of Mother-of-Pearl can be replaced with pieces of broken gaming counters.

Oil Lamps

To strengthen the mantle and make it last longer, soak it in a small jar of vinegar for 10 minutes. Dry well before using.

Rings and Stains Caused by Heat, Alcohol, or Water

Use cigarette or cigar ash mixed with saliva. Rub it into the mark with a finger covered in a clean soft cloth. Finish off with camphor, linseed, or olive oil mixed with fine pumice powder.

To Unstop a Jammed Decanter

Warm the neck of the decanter to make it expand a little. Add a few drops of oil around the stopper and gently twist out.

Small chips in the glass can be rubbed down with a fine dry emery paper.

Parchment

Do not attempt to repair very old parchment. It needs an expert. If a parchment has been folded for many years it is possible to flatten it. Damp the creases at the back over the spout of a steaming pan. Do not let the parchment get too wet. Lay it on clean blotting paper, with another sheet of blotting paper on top and then flatten it with an even weight.

Embedded Screws
Where they have become rusted into wood or metal, carefully place 2 drops of olive oil around the screw and heat the screw-head with the very hot end of a file. The heat makes the screw expand and the cooling that follows causes it to contract and free itself.

POLISHING

The oldest polish is beeswax. Shred the beeswax into a bowl, pour in turpentine, and place the bowl in a pan of hot water (never over a naked flame) until the mixture melts. Remove from heat and keep in a closed tin. It should be the consistency of softish butter.

To Make a French Polish
5–6 oz of shellac dissolved in 1 pint of methylated spirit.

Linseed Oil Varnish
For dressing and polishing wood furniture. Impregnate wood with a mixture of linseed oil and turpentine. (Turpentine is a natural oily sap from a type of pine tree.)

Burnish the surface of the wood with fine brick dust on a cork rubber. (Mixed with shellac, this is also used as coach varnish.)

Wax Polish

For furniture. Shred 1 lb of beeswax and pack lightly into a double boiler. Add enough turpentine to cover the flakes of wax and add a salt-spoonful of ivory black for each pound of mixture. Heat slowly, stir occasionally. When mixture becomes liquid, pour it into a bowl to cool and harden. Use before it gets too hard.

Mirror and Glass Polish

Keep used tea leaves for several days. Re-infuse them with boiled water and strain. Use this to polish mirrors, glasses, and varnished wood.

Veneers

Some veneered furniture gets too much sunlight. Avoid cracks and blisters by rubbing the wood occasionally with a silk cloth dipped in warm linseed oil.

Candle Polish

For floor polish. Old candle-ends make good floor polish.
Melt down the candles in a bowl standing in hot water
(never over a naked flame). Remove the wicks and add
turpentine in equal proportion. Warm slightly before
using.

Against Water Humidity

Leave small containers of water hung on the back of
large heavy vases, so they cannot be seen. This stops the
furniture in the room drying out in the summertime.

GENERAL HOUSEHOLD TIPS

Chandling (Making Candles)

Making candles was a regular chore
for the Kitchen Maids. Candles were
made using a wick, made of dried
stripped rushes, repeatedly dipped
individually into hot beef fat or
marrow bone grease (drying them
between applications).

These long reed candles, bundled
together in long holders, provided good
lighting. However, they only lasted about an
hour, so constantly had to be replaced.

Soap Balls

An old recipe, very popular in the eighteen century:

Take a pound of fine white Castile sope. Shave it thin in a pinte of Rose-water, & let it stand for 2 or 3 days. Then pour all the water from it, & put to it halfe a pinte of fresh water, & so let it stand for 1 day. Then pour out that liquid, & put half a pinte more, & let it stand a night more. Then put to it halfe an ounce of powdered Sweet Marjoram, a quarter of an ounce of powdered Winter Savory, 2 or 3 drops of Oyl of Spike, & the Oyl of Cloves, 3 grains of Musk, & 3 grains of Ambergris.

Work all together in a fair mortar with the Powder of a dryed Almond Cake (already beaten as small as fine flowre), So roll it round in the hands in Rose Water.

Making Animal-Glue

Made from animal bones and skins, starch, fish offal, and the sap of trees, it was used in all woodwork. The glue has to be prepared in a water-jacketed gluepot, and must not be allowed to boil (or it will turn dark and stain the wood). Glue must be heated on application, and the wood joint has to be warmed up in a warm room for 2 days before. Allow 24 hours to dry the joint.

Household Coal Tip

Coal will burn longer if sprinkled with a solution of water and washing soda (4 pints of water to a small handful of soda). Be careful to let the coal dry thoroughly before use.

1 Nasturtiums are edible and can be used alongside marigolds, pansies and bergamot in salads. (© Mally Francis)

2 Dandelion can be used in cough syrup. It can also be used in stock, soup, salad, chutney, tea, wine, mead and ale. (© Mally Francis)

3 The opium poppy. Poppy petals boiled in water can be used to combat dry, wrinkly skin. (© Mally Francis)

4 Roses. It takes 2,000 roses to make one 10ml bottle of rose water. (© Mally Francis)

5 Strawberries, when mashed with cucumber, make a soothing paste to combat puffy eyes. (© Mally Francis)

6 Olives. Sore lips can be treated with honey and a little olive oil. (© Mally Francis)

7 Sunflower. Sprouting sunflower seeds should be eaten to treat acne. (© Mally Francis)

8 Berries and rosehips. Oils for healing and scent can be extracted from many flowers, leaves, fruit, peel, seeds, wood, bark, and roots. (© Mally Francis)

9 Mallow and ivy-leafed bluebell. Mallow was said to be useful in the treatment of rickets or weakness in the joints. (© Mally Francis)

10 Thistles and creeping cinque. A thistle and milk hot drink at bedtime can cleanse the system. (© Mally Francis)

11 Rhododendron can be used for textile dyes. Combined with iron it makes a light green dye; combined with alum and tin it makes a lemon dye; and to make a dark green dye combine it with alum, iron and copper sulphate. (© Mally Francis)

12 Sweet peas. Pot-pourri can be made with these when combined with honeysuckle, rose petals, lavender, rosemary and thyme. (© Mally Francis)

For Worms

of Myrrh, Aloes, & Mithendale, each a g.rs of an
a little Powder of dryd wormwood, mix these into a paste with
fresh ox or Balls gall & spread it upon sheeps Leather
lay it upon the persons stomach with the point upward
& the bottom not to touch the navell by a fingers breadth,
when it has lain for 24 hours let the person take some
Physick every other day for three times, & about 10
days after a dose rather stronger, let the Plaister
lye on as long as it will stick, if it makes the
stomach itch & break not into like spots, lay the
skin of mutton suet on when you take the plaister
of — the above Quantity of Ingredients will spread
a great many Plaisters, but it must not be used
with gall till you use it; if the person is too weak
to take Physick let them have the following Glister
every day or every other day as you judge proper for a
mans dose (the Glister wormwood & wormseed of each half an
ounce this is enough for 3 Glisters) boile it in thin
Gruel or small broth, when enough, put in a spoonfull
of course brown than strain it & give a grown Child half a
pint — — more in proportion to the Age.
The person or child must not eat Milk or fruit
so long as the Plaister lye on.
It will not stick if the person has not worms.

The
Shape of the
Plaister — leave a
margin when you spread
it, as this paper is marked,
the size must be according
to the person, this paper is
proper for a child of about
8 years old.

Miss Plowden's receit for ye Collek or ye que 37

Take one of Chamemile flowers, & one drechm of salt
of Wormwhod, half an ounce of Brod string Bill...
this together in a Pint of boylin water, & drink
all about an hower before you expect a fitt...

A receipt for ye Dropsie — 38
Take ye branck leaves of Artichoques, & pound in a morter
... strain ye liquer into a bottle & keep it till
you have a fitt of the Dropsie then tak a spoonfull or more
... twice a day morning & after noon, it will purge
you may repeat it as ye see occasion &c.

Ri: Bell Dav receip for ye yallow or black Jaunders 39
take fanerick turmeryrick & inward Bark of Barbery
... pouder, sift then three a siver a peny worth ground small
... steel fast for a time after you drink it, repeat it as oft as
you have occasion &c.

The Rume plaisters — 40
Take troo pennyworth of soft B wee galary pitch one
pennyworth of venes turpentine as much more...
your fist, melt all these to gether in an Earthen Cuppe,
& keep it for use, then you must apply this plaisters on
bouth your temples, it will stop the rume from...

A water for sore Eyes — 41
Take an ounce of sweet fennel seeds, and a handful of
kyssop, put these into five half pints of spring water,
& boyl in together, till one half is wasted, then strain,
it off, when you use it warm, a little of this water in a
spoon, & wit a fine soft linnen rag bath ye Eyes as soon as
you awake in ye morning, & so as oft times in ye day & when
you go to Bead likewise,

14 Miss Plowden's recipes.

15 The description of a Dairy Maid's duties, written by Martha Davenport.

three

M'Lady's Garden

TIPS FOR PLANTING

1. Plant herbs under the full phase of the moon.
2. Do not use the left hand, or the devil's work will ensue, for herbs have mystical properties.

Parsley
Takes a long time to germinate because it goes nine times to the devil before it emerges. Grow in rich soil.

Garlic and Chives
Prevents blackspot in roses when planted around the rose-bed.

Mint
Put sprigs of mint on cabbages in garden to keep cabbage white caterpillars away.

Marigolds
Plant them among tomatoes to keep whitefly at bay.

How to Make Compost for Containers
Put a layer of stones into a 14in tub and then put in a few sheets of crimpled newspaper. Top this up with compost – and your geraniums will bloom throughout the summer.

How to Get Better Yields
Grow hyssop to attract bees into the garden. Rub beehives with balm to keep the bees at home.

A Scented Garden Seat

❦

Build a raised box 1½ feet high. Fill with soil and plant it up with
chamomile. This makes a fragrant seat.

❦

HERB PLANTING

For the Cook's Garden

alecost	corn salad	nettle
angelica	cumin	oregano
basil	dill	parsley
bay	fennel	purslane
borage	French sorrel	rosemary
bistort	garlic	sage
caraway	lovage	savory
chicory	lemon balm	shallot
chervil	marjoram	tarragon
chives	marigold	thyme
coriander	mint	

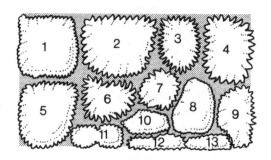

Plan for Planting Small Cook's Garden

1. fennel
2. rosemary
3. tarragon
4. angelica
5. sage
6. marjoram
7. lemon balm
8. sorrel
9. mint
10. thyme
11. savory
12. chives
13. parsley

Plan for Planting Decorative Herb Garden:

1. thymes (various)
2. marjoram
3. sage
4. eau de cologne mint
5. angelica
6. chives
7. sweet cicely
8. tarragon
9. parsley
10. thymes (various)
11. purple sage
12. lemon balm
13. spearmint
14. fennel
15. basil
16. parsley
17. savory
18. apple mint
19. thymes
20. marjoram

21. savory
22. parsley
23. purslane
24. lemon balm
25. chives
26. lovage
27. apple mint
28. poppy
29. basil
30. thymes (various)
31. parsley
32. cumin
33. corn salad
34. marigold
35. rosemary
36. sage (narrow leaf)
37. sorrel
38. sweet cicely
39. Bowles' mint
40. pennyroyal
41. thrift

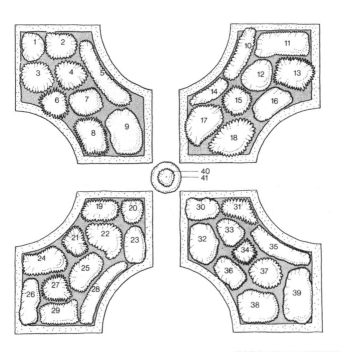

Planting Herbs for the Blind
(Textured and scented leaves)

angelica	mints
alecost	pennyroyal
bergamot	rosemary
chamomile	rue
feverfew	sage
geraniums	southernwood
lavender	sweet cicely
lemon balm	tansy
lily-of-the-valley	thymes
meadowsweet	wormwood
mignonette	

PEST-FREE PLANTING – HERBS WITH VEGETABLES

The herb aromas and secretions deter pests, and some greatly improve the flavour of the vegetables.

General List of Companion Herbs (planted in the same plot)

Asparagus: basil, tarragon

Beans: rosemary, sage, tarragon – (not garlic or chives)

Broccoli: chamomile, peppermint, dill, rosemary, chives, tarragon

Cabbages: mint, nasturtiums, dill, rosemary, oregano, chives, chamomile, sage, thyme

Carrots: chives, rosemary, sage, tarragon – (not dill)

Celery: tarragon – (not dill)

Cucumbers: nasturtiums, oregano, chamomile, tarragon – (not sage)

Fennel: tarragon – (not coriander)

Garlic: tarragon

Lettuces: dill, tarragon

Onions/Leeks: chamomile, tarragon

Peas: parsley, rosemary, tarragon – (not chives)

Potatoes: coriander, oregano – (not rosemary)

Pumpkins: nasturtiums, oregano, tarragon – (not sage)

Radishes: nasturtiums, tarragon

Tomatoes: basil, mint, nasturtiums, parsley, chives, oregano – (not dill)

The Three Top Deterrents
Chives and coriander planted with all vegetables (but not beans): keeps away aphids

Garlic: keeps away Japanese beetles

Sage planted with cabbage and carrots: keeps away cabbage moths and carrot flies

⇥ *WARNING* ⇤

Some combinations can be harmful. The worst is dill with tomatoes, which will attract the tomato horn worm, which destroys all the crop.

FAVOURITE HERBS AND FLOWERS AROUND THE HOUSE

Tarragon: makes tarragon vinegar to flavour salad dressings and mustard, butter and sauces, eggs, fish, meat and poultry.

Costmary (or alecost): their dried leaves make good bookmarks.

Borage: a favourite … young leaves fried in pancake batter.

Summer savoury: rub their leaves on bee stings for relief.

Rue: wear a sprig of rue when weeding in summer. It wards off flies.

Flower Petals for Salads

Use blooms of pot marigolds, pansies, polyanthus, bergamot, hyssop and nasturtiums. All edible.

M' Lady's Garden

USEFUL WILD HERBS

They are for immediate fresh use as required:

Chickweed: a creeping ground-covering plant that comes up in cleared ground in the spring. Rich in vitamins.

Cleavers: abundant sticky creeper. Leave a patch to grow over a wall or fence. Used as a spring tonic.

Dandelion: cheerful self-seeding plant. with yellow flowers in the spring and summer. The leaves are full of vitamins and minerals.

Nettles: they grow in poor soil. When cooked, they are full of iron and minerals. Use like spinach.

Yarrow: grassland weed with astringent properties. Keep at hand to stop bleeding.

And most important: you must have an elder tree – a 'cure-all' described as 'the poor man's medicine'.

four

Servants

r Mansel Talbot (from Lacock Abbey) of Margam and Penrice wrote to a cousin in 1794 asking for advice on the correct terms and conditions for taking on 'Servants In Livery' prior to his marriage to Lady Mary Strangeways:

I don't at first mean to trouble myself with more than 3 servants in livery: viz William, an under butler & a handy boy. The coachman & old Mr Williams to wait at table besides, occasionally, & also the postillion if wanted.

I have hitherto given William 14 guineas, a full suit of livery, a fustian frock, breeches, a grey jacket & waistcoat, a greatcoat once in 2 years, & a round hat laid. With 2 guineas extra for boots & breeches.

To my coachman I give 25 guineas a year, full livery, stable waistcoat, laid jacket & waistcoat; & 3 guineas for boots & breeches.

To the postillion, a laid jacket & waistcoat, a plain frock & stable waistcoat with fustian breeches; also 3 guineas a year for boots & breeches.

Is this right or should more be given?

Pray, Sir, say & you'll oblige me much…

Although this seems to be a small staff for a large house, this would have included an army of un-liveried indoor staff (cook, housemaids, laundry maids, scullery maids etc.). Also, his bride-to-be, Lady Mary Strangeways, would probably have brought her own personal servants with her.

SERVANTS' AGES

Typical ages for indoor staff:

Butler 40–60
Footman 25
Under Footman 18

Housekeeper 45
Head Housemaid 30
Under Housemaid 18
Laundry Maid 20–30

Cook 35–60
Kitchen Maid 19
Scullery Maid 18
Parlour Maid 23

Lady's Maid 35

Groom 30–50
Stable Boys 18–25

They would come from all over the country, hoping to learn their trade and seek advancement, studying under a top-class Housekeeper, Cook, or Butler. Their employer's excellent references were essential to climbing the domestic ladder.

The Butler, Cook, and Housekeeper usually had a suite of rooms of their own, and sometimes they had their own family installed (especially from the late nineteenth century onwards).

A large house, like Castletown, had a dedicated wing for servants, with the maids' (young girls) sleeping quarters deliberated separated from the footmen's (young men).

INTRODUCTION TO THE LIVES OF SERVANTS

Whilst history inevitably tends to focus on the high-profile lords and ladies, influential individuals who are well documented in historical archives, it is vital not to forget the equally-important millions of ordinary people who worked long, arduous hours, day in and day out to ensure the smooth running of their masters' castles and houses. For every one Lord of the Manor, there might be an army of fifty working on the land and in the household.

The contribution of the many and various servants and household staff must also be acknowledged. These people were not simply faceless minions; they were all individual personalities, with their own unique stories to tell. This

section, therefore, attempts to allow a glimpse into these lives and into the day-to-day running of the Weddington Castle estate.

SERVANTS' DUTIES

The Housekeeper

Always referred to as 'Mrs' by the other servants, whether she was married or not, the housekeeper was second-in-command of the household and was the immediate representative of her mistress.

Advance orders for each day were passed down according to the number of visitors expected and the necessary bedrooms to be prepared.

She was responsible for the ordering of domestic goods from the tradesmen, usually a week in advance, and was required to have an understanding of accounts, keeping daily, neat, accurate and precise household domestic accounts for every house expense as well as the tradesmen's bills. These accounts were balanced and examined by the mistress monthly.

The housekeeper was in charge of the household linens and kept the inventory, making sure the family and staff always had a clean supply of linens and bedding. She organised the constant mending of sheets and pillowcases, and made sure the laundry was ironed, pressed and folded to her taste. She also had the responsibility of overseeing the cleaning and polishing of all the household furniture, and ordered some of the specialised ingredients from abroad.

The housekeeper was responsible for the inventory of other household necessities such as soap, candles, sugar, flour and spices. She negotiated with the cook for the needs of the kitchen. She supervised the china closet, and the stillroom, where cordials and preserves were made and stored.

She had considerable knowledge of herbs, and would instruct the gardeners to grow lavender, lemon verbena etc. to be dried, made into bags, and constantly replaced amongst the linens and in visitors' cupboards.

All the Maids

Under the supervision of the Housekeeper, there was several house maid positions, including Parlour Maids, Chamber Maids, Laundry Maids, Still-Room Maids, 'Between Maids' – these maids performed double-duty as both kitchen and housemaids – and Maid-of-all-Work. These were the employees who really maintained the house.

Each had their own set of duties and responsibilities, which included: lighting and stoking the fires; providing clean, hot water for washing and bathing, and removing the dirty water four times a day (before breakfast, at noon, before dinner and at bedtime); empting and cleaning chamber pots; thoroughly cleaning all the public rooms of the house; scrubbing floors; sweeping ashes; cleaning and polishing grates, candlesticks, marble floors and all the furniture; brushing carpets and beating rugs; and washing mountains of laundry (which needed to be soaked, blued, washed, rinsed, rinsed again, wrung out, hung to dry, and then ironed).

The Housemaid

The Housemaid's work was more back-breaking and exhausting than we can imagine now. There were lamps to clean and fill every day, and because the working area was in the basement, maids frequently had to lug hot water up to the third floor of the house where the bedrooms were. In addition, in order to tend the fires and keep them lit, a maid had to carry scuttles or buckets of coal up each flight of stairs to all the fireplaces in the house.

Indeed, the Housemaid's day was long, intensive and painfully strenuous. It began at 6 a.m. when she rose and dressed, then made tea for the Lady's Maid and the Housekeeper, serving them by 6.30 a.m. She worked on until 10.30 or 11 at night (sometimes later), when she could finally retire for the night with the house completely in order and ready for her to start all over again the following day.

Young Housemaids were usually village girls, often brought up in the district where they worked. Typically, they were plucked from a struggling family with no facilities at home, and were considered fortunate to be offered a life of service in 'the Big House'.

A kindly Housekeeper allocated an older, experienced maid to 'mother' her when she first arrived, to show her the ropes; for a new recruit felt lonely, and cast into a land of terrifying rules and constant reproach. She soon learnt that when she was on duty M'Lord and M'Lady expected her to be both unseen and unheard.

What did new Housemaids think of the grand houses they found themselves in? It could well have been an alien planet. Everything was strange for them, including their first use of the servants' toilet. Many a girl was convinced that sitting on a toilet seat where a young male Footman had just been would undoubtedly make her pregnant.

In the late 1800s, they saw strange sights like the wonders of gas or electric light for the first time; though part of them must have regretted the passing of the era of candlelight – for now every dark recess was illuminated, and so had to be cleaned and had to pass daily inspection by the Housekeeper.

The Parlour Maid

She would be washed and dressed by 6 a.m. to begin her duties, which included sweeping and dusting the drawing rooms, dining room, front hall, and other sitting-rooms, as well as cleaning the ashes from the grates and lighting the fires.

She cleaned the lamps and polished the candlesticks, carried up the large jugs of hot water to the bedrooms, made the other servants' beds, tidied the rooms and cleaned the front staircase.

She brought breakfast in bed to the lady of the house and often to elderly female visitors as well. While the rest of the household was at breakfast downstairs, she made the beds, dusted underneath, shook the curtains, cleaned dirty marks on carpets, furniture or walls, and lit the fires.

Each bedroom would need to be supplied with soap, candles, clean towels, and writing paper.

The Parlour Maid would have to answer the bell at all times.

On special days their work might also include: cleaning the knives, rubbing up table silver, tiding the pantry, getting dressed for serving luncheon, clearing away luncheon, washing up table silver, filling coal scuttles as needed, preparing guest rooms, turning down the beds in the evenings, taking up and filling the jugs with hot water again, closing the curtains, and tidying the bedrooms for night-time.

The Kitchen Maid

The Kitchen Maids and Scullery Maids assisted the Cook, following her instructions all day. If they fed twenty in the dining room twice a day when they had visitors, their hours started at 6 a.m., and did not finish until 11 p.m.

They lit the kitchen fires early in the morning and kept the kitchen and all its pots and pans clean for Cook's constant use during the day. They also kept the larders clean and helped Cook make the preserves. They chopped and prepared all the food ingredients and provided the necessary elbow-grease for mixing batters, sauces, cakes and fillings.

When there were a lot of visitors in the house, the senior Kitchen Maid frequently cooked meals for other servants, while Cook focused her attention on provisions for the household 'above stairs'.

The Laundry Maid
In large country houses, the Laundry Maid's duty was the sorting and washing of the family's fine cotton, linen and muslins. This was a situation of great importance at a time when the washing was all done at home.

Considerable room was laid out for the laundry area. There would have been a washhouse, an ironing and drying room with pulleys and racks dangling from the ceiling, and sometimes a drying-closet heated by the furnaces. The washhouse was often attached to the kitchen with all its fumes and steam, but gradually this fashion was found impractical. A funnel or shaft was built into the wall to carry away the laundry steam.

There was also a bleaching-house adjoining which was a second room of about the same size, used for ironing, drying and mangling with wringing-out rollers. This room had an ironing board opposite to the light, with a set of several hand-held flat-irons lined up for alternate use. These were heated on a hot-plate built into the chimney, with a furnace beneath it and a flue for carrying the hot air around the room for drying – as soon as one iron cooled, another was hot and ready for use. If a too-hot iron was used, the precious linen was ruined. Keeping all the irons at the correct temperature was an art.

The room also contained a strong white deal table, about 12 or 14 feet long and about 3½ feet broad, with drawers for ironing blankets. A mangle stood in one corner near a sink and both hanging and free-standing clothes-horses were used for the drying and airing. There was also a cupboard for tidying away the irons, starch, and the blueing for the whites.

The Laundry Maid commenced her work on Monday mornings with a careful examination of the washing committed to her care, and carefully entered every item into the Wash Book; separating the white linen and collars, sheets, and body-linen into one heap; fine muslins into another; coloured cottons and linen fabric into a third; woollens into a fourth; and the rougher kitchen and other greasy cloths into a fifth pile.

Every item had to be examined for stains, ink, grease-spots, fruit stains, or wine stains. After examination and sorting, the sheets and fine linen was placed in one of the large tubs and just covered in lukewarm water in which a little soda had been dissolved and mixed. It was left there to soak until the following morning.

Early on the Tuesday morning, the fires were lit and as soon as the hot water was ready, the washing started. The sheets and the body-linen were dealt with first. As each article was removed from their soaking tub it was rinsed, rubbed, wrung, and laid aside until the tub was empty, when the dirty water is drawn off.

After this first washing, the linen was placed into a second water as hot as the hand could bear, and rubbed over again. Each item was re-examined for spots not yet removed, which required to be soaped again, and rubbed until thoroughly clean; then they were rinsed and wrung-out – the larger and stronger items by two of the women; the smaller and more delicate articles required gentler treatment.

Wash-day was concluded by rinsing the tubs, cleaning the coppers, scrubbing the floors of the wash-house, and restoring everything to order and cleanliness.

Thursday and Friday were the mangling, starching, and ironing days.

The Lady's Maid

The Lady's Maid, in a medium-sized family house, was hired by, and reported directly to, the mistress of the house, rather than the Housekeeper.

Because her position necessitated a close proximity to her mistress, the Lady's Maid was often mistrusted and generally disliked by the lower servants, who possibly felt that she was haughty, or might 'tattle-tale' on them.

Often, this treatment of the Lady's Maid caused her to feel isolated, as if she did not fit into either world. Her position allowed privileges of comfort and luxury not enjoyed by the lower servants, yet no matter how high-ranking her position was, her station remained among the 'poor domestic servants'.

To qualify for the position, a Lady's Maid was to be neat in appearance, have strong verbal skills, be pleasant, be able to read and write well, be proficient with her needle and handiwork. Honesty was an absolute necessity, as the Lady's Maid would be handling her mistress' clothing, jewellery and personal items, and she would be expected to tell the truth, without gossiping.

The daily duties of the Lady's Maid included helping her mistress dress and undress, and maintaining her mistress' wardrobe, including laundering the most delicate items and using her dressmaking skills to create new articles of clothing for any and all occasions. In addition, the Lady's Maid prepared beauty lotions for her mistress' delicate skin, and styled her mistress' hair.

But the role of an elite Lady's Maid, working in one of the grand country houses, was very much more extensive. It was a coveted position, and she had a great deal of influence. Her skills as an apothecary, a beautician, and her considerable gardening knowledge, were vital to her mistress. She was able to order the gardener how and where to grow her special plants and herbs, so she could make her secret brews and concoctions for daily administration. She had the daily health and well-being of all female members of the family in her charge.

There is clear evidence of very personal procedures done by the Lady's Maid to her mistress, some with extremely invasive overtones (like 'M'Lady's Full Body Skin-Brushing Regime' on p. 41), which nowadays seems more like torture. Some of the 'Anti-Ageing Exercises' prove the

Lady's Maid even dictated her mistress' sleeping habits. The rigorous beauty regimes of the time were harsh and time-consuming – all dominated and ordered by the Lady's Maid.

A Lady's Maid would only come by personal recommendation from a friend. Any employer would be sensible to choose her Lady's Maid wisely.

The Dairy Maid

Transcript of Dairy Maid's duties in a smaller household, written by Martha Davenport (see plate section for the original manuscript):

My dairy maid is to:

Look after 2 or 3 cows if I have so many, in every respect which I shall direct.

She is to look after the swine, to feed constantly every day of the week, excepting the day she washes the sope washing and that day my housemaid does it for her & likewise takes on my powltrey, for that day, which place I expect to be kept very clean and they fed 3 or 4 times a day by ye dairy maid and those that are in ye coops, and when they are killed to pick them. Those about the yard once or twice a day to feed them.

She is to get up with the laindry maid of a Monday night generally to wash her sope washing and goes through out with all that business till the laundry maid goes to bed.

She is to buck of the Wednesday, & wash it of the Thursday once a fortnight & has one to help her wash the bucking.

Of a Fryday once a fortnight, unless upon extraordinary occasion I should see occasion to scower oftener, she is to go through out with the cook in scowering the pewter & brass & coper.

She is to help the housemaid to make all the beds, to clean Mrs Finches room, her own, the passage chamber, one pair of stairs and the servants hall.

She is to bake brown bread every week.

To help the cook in the kitchen every 3rd Sunday & to wash the dishes that day & help in the kitchen when any company dines here.

She is to make Mr Wooleys bed and the mens and clean those two rooms.

To clean the copper cans, sestern and plate ring every other day & the wooden bottles.

When the pigs are killed to help wash and clear the pudding
and look after them till cook is ready fir them.

She is to clean the seats at church once a week.

To help Mrs Finch in everything that she shall order her to do
and never to go out without her leave or mine.

She is expected to get up very early in the morning and keep
very good hours at night.

Of a Monday to help mend the household linning or when
any is to be made to help like way.

To lay the servants hall tablecloth at these meals.

She is to dispute nothing I or Finch directed her to do in
general.

The Cook

A professional cook would not do any general house cleaning, nor any 'plain cooking', and her ingredients would generally be prepared for her by the kitchen staff.

The busiest times of the day for the cook were mornings and early evenings. In the morning hours, Cook would first meet with the mistress of the house for her to review and approve menus, then she would prepare soup for the following day, as soup was 'not usually meant to be eaten

the same day it was made'. Next, Cook would prepare
the jellies, pastries, creams and entrees required for the
evening meal, and luncheon was prepared for those
'above stairs'. The afternoon hours might allow Cook a
little respite, unless guests were staying in the house or if
a dinner party was to be held; on such occasions as these,
servants found no time for rest.

The hours between 5 p.m. and 10 p.m. were extremely
hectic for Cook. Once dinner had been served, Cook's
work for the day was finished, and the remainder of
the cleaning up and chores fell to the Kitchen and the
Scullery Maids. These remaining chores were extremely
laborious, as a full dinner for eighteen people could
easily produce some 500 separate items of china,
glassware, kitchenware and cutlery that needed to
be cleaned.

The 'Plain Cook', unlike the aforementioned 'Professed Cook', would have general housekeeping duties to perform, many of which were not related to cooking at all, especially in households where there were no Kitchen or Scullery Maids. She might be expected to dust and sweep the dining room or parlour, light the fires, sweep the front hall and/ or door-step, and even clean the grates – all in addition to maintaining the work of the kitchen. She would need to rise early – 6 a.m. in the summer months and 6.30 a.m. in the winter – to light the kitchen fire and then complete all her work upstairs before cooking breakfast. Plain Cooks were usually expected to cook simple meals. For example, for luncheon she might serve a joint of meat, vegetables and pudding. For dinner, she would prepare much the same meal, or might vary it by serving fish, vegetables, potatoes and tarts.

Following dinner, the Plain Cook would need to clean the dishes, scour tables and kitchen counters, and perhaps mop the kitchen floor so that it would be clean for the next morning. These were all tasks that the Scullery Maid would typically perform, but in a household where there was no Scullery Maid, these chores were left to the Plain Cook. Finally, it was her responsibility to see that the kitchen fires had burnt low, that the gas (in homes that had gas) in the kitchen and passages was turned off, and that the basement doors and windows were securely fastened. At last, she could retire for the night.

The Butler

The Butler wore gentlemen's period-fashions. He was often a distinguished figure of a man with an imposing presence, who demanded respect from his subordinates. The list of duties required by the Butler varied with the position and status of his employer.

In smaller households, the Butler's work was fairly difficult. He hired and dismissed the lower staff (male), and he was personally responsible for their conduct. He was to ensure that all the work of the staff ran smoothly and that any issues were quickly handled.

If the house contained a plate room, it was usually located near the Butler's pantry. Each night the Butler would need to be sure it was securely locked. Either the Butler or the Footman was expected to sleep nearby, as guard. In the morning the Butler passed out the pieces of plate that needed to be cleaned, and occasionally he cleaned them himself, at the same time he cleaned the household's ornamental items of silver.

The Butler was responsible for the arrangement of the dining room table and the announcing of dinner. Together with the Footmen, he waited at table. It was the Butler's job to carve the joint of meat and to remove the covers from other dishes. He served wine and set out each additional course. While dessert was being enjoyed the Butler made sure that the drawing room – where the family would retreat for coffee – was in order. He made sure that lamps or candles were lit and that the fire was warmly glowing. He then returned to his pantry and awaited the ring of the bell, which signalled he may return to the company. He would then announce that the drawing room was ready. Once the family had settled into the drawing room, the Butler would hand around cups and saucers, while the Footman followed behind carrying a pot of coffee.

The Butler's final tasks of the day were to see that all doors and windows were locked, that the plate was safely secured, and that all the fires in the house were safe.

The Footman / Postillion

Directly below the Butler was the Footman. His position was multifarious, and included a wide variety of duties that ranged from accompanying the mistress in her carriage as she paid calls or went shopping, to polishing the household copper and plate; or from waiting at table, to cleaning knives, cutlery, shoes and boots.

Other duties of the Footman (who was frequently referred to as 'James' or 'John', no matter what his real name might have been), would have included acting as M'Lady's personal Footman. That is, among his other duties, he would have prepared her early morning breakfast tray, cleaned her shoes, brushed any mud off her

dress hems and riding habits, paid small charges of her travelling expenses such as toll gates and handsome cabs (he could reclaim these expenses from the Housekeeper), and if she owned a dog he would be the one to take it for a walk. He would also accompany her when she went out in the carriage, sitting on the box with the coachman (then in later days, with the chauffeur), and would open and close for her the carriage door, as well as the door to any stores she entered, unless there was already a doorman. He waited for her return, carried any packages for her, and once he helped her back into the carriage, he covered her knees with a blanket or fur rug. When the mistress went calling and no one was at home, she waited in the carriage while the Footman left her visiting card at the front door.

In earlier days, a Postillion rode on one of the two carriage horses, but latterly the Footmen liked to call themselves Postilions, even though they only rode on the outside of the coach.

The Footman also acted as a valet to the eldest son, and sometimes to the master himself. He was responsible for laying the luncheon table. Other general duties of the Footman included cleaning all the mirrors, carrying wood and coal, trimming lamps, running errands, lighting the house at dusk, cleaning silver and gold, answering the drawing room and/or parlour bells, announcing visitors, waiting at dinner, attending the gentlemen in the smoking room following dinner, and attending in the front hall as dinner guests were leaving.

Because of their public exposure at dinner and to guests, Footmen were expected to be the most presentable of the male servants. In addition to there being an 'ideal height' requirement for Footmen, they were also assessed on their appearance in 'full livery' (uniform), which for outdoors consisted of an ornate tail coat, knee breeches, stockings, white gloves, buckled shoes and powdered hair with cocked hat. For indoors their livery was sometimes a bit less formal. Instead of a tail coat and buckled shoes, they usually wore a dress coat and pumps. Later in the century it was more common to see a uniform of white tie and tails with brass buttons that were stamped with the family crest or arms.

The Groom

The Groom's first duties were to keep his horses in good condition, but he was sometimes expected to perform the duties of a valet, to ride out with his master, on occasions, to wait at table, and otherwise assist in the house: in these cases, he would need to have the means of dressing himself, and keeping his clothes entirely away from the stables.

In the morning, about six o'clock, or soon thereafter, the stables would be opened and the horses fed, by cleaning the rack and throwing in fresh hay, putting it lightly in the rack, that the horses may get it out easily; a short time afterwards their usual morning feed of oats should be put into the manger. While this is going on, the Stable Boy had been removing the horse dung and sweeping and

washing out the stables, both of which would be done every day, with every corner carefully swept in order to keep the stable sweet and clean.

The real duties of the Groom follow: where the horses are not taken out for early exercise, the work of grooming immediately commences. Having tied up the horse's head, he takes a currycomb and curries him all over the body, to raise the dust, beginning first at the neck, holding the left cheek of the head-collar in the left hand, and curries him from the setting-on of his head all over the body to the rump, down to the point of the hock; then the Groom changes his hands, and curries him all over his back, joining his right side to his left, and currying him all under the belly near the fore-bowels, and so all over from the knees and back upwards; after that, he goes to the far side and does that likewise.

Then the Groom takes a dead horse's tail, or failing that, a cotton dusting-cloth, and strikes away that which the currycomb has raised. Then he takes a round brush made of bristles, with a leather handle, and dresses the horse all over, head, body, and legs, to the very fetlocks, always cleaning the brush from the dust by rubbing it with the currycomb. In the curry-combing process (and with general brushing) it must be applied with mildness, especially with fine-skinned horses, otherwise the tickling irritates them much. The brushing is succeeded by a hair-cloth, with which the Groom rubs him all over again very hard, both to take away loose hairs and lay his coat; then the Groom washes his hands in water and rubs him all over while they are wet, as well over the head as the body.

Lastly, the Groom takes a clean cloth, and rubs him all over again till he be dry; then he takes another hair-cloth, and rubs all his legs exceedingly well from the knees and hocks downwards to his hoofs, picking and dressing them very carefully about the fetlocks, so as to remove all gravel and dust which will sometimes lie in the bending of the joints. In addition to this practice, modern Grooms add wisping, which usually follows brushing. The best wisp is made from a hay-band, untwisted, and again double up after being moistened with water: this is applied to every part of the body, as the brushing has been, by changing the hands, taking care in all these operations to carry the hand in the direction of the coat. Stains on the hair are removed by sponging, or, when the coat is very dirty, by the water-brush; The whole being finished off by a linen or flannel cloth. The horse-rug should now be put on by taking the cloth in both hands, with the outside next to you, and, with the right hand to the off side, throw it over his back, placing it no farther back than will leave it straight and level, which will be about a foot from the tail. Put the roller girth around the horse below the withers, check it is laying smoothly on both sides. The horse now has his tail combed out, and cleaned of stains with a wet brush or sponge, trimming both tail and mane, and forelock when necessary, smoothing them down with a brush on which a little oil has been dropped.

five

Food and Cookery

The cookery books from the archives of many historic houses like Castletown and Lacock Abbey illustrate the wide diversity of food available during the seventeen and eighteenth centuries. As well as the familiar meats of today – beef, lamb, pork, veal and mutton – much use was made of sweetbreads, calf's heads, sheep's tongues, pig's feet and tongue. There was a dedicated game larder, which provided venison, hare, rabbit, partridge, pigeons, teal, quail, snipe, widgeons and woodcock. Dishes of chicken, turkey, duck and goose (with their giblets) also appeared at table.

Fish was a staple part of the eighteenth- and early nineteenth-century diet. There are recipes for the stewing of carp and eels, of how to roast a large pike, and how to bake fresh herrings in vinegar and wine, very similar to the soused herring of today. The estates had their own stew ponds and small canals with their own lock systems. These were naturally fed with fresh streams constantly running in and out. These were kept well stocked with different sorts of fish, like carp and tench. The pike and eel, especially, needed to be kept under a controlling watch.

Food generally seemed to be stewed or boiled – stewed pigeon, stewed rump of beef, a ragout of giblets, stewed cabbage, boiled spinach with cream, for example.

The oven was used chiefly to cook rolls, cakes, and small biscuits. Mushrooms were broiled in a grid-iron, and a large pike roasted on a spit encased in a basket of split sticks to prevent it falling apart.

A great deal of food was preserved to provide variety out of season. There were home-made wines, including orange, cherry, cowslip, sage, elder, birch, raisin, ginger, and quince, along with traditional mead and metheglin. Cheeses were made often as a speciality to each house.

Houses with rivers and streams usually built 'Ice Houses' by hollowing out a cavern by the bank, where ice broken up from the water was stored for use to preserve meat and also to chill wines during the summer.

THE BREWERY

Until the late nineteenth century, beer was a safer drink than either water or milk. The process of boiling and fermenting to make the beer killed many harmful bugs.

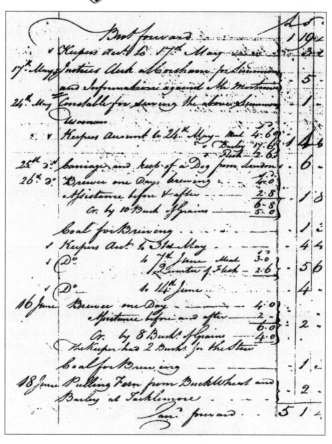

Brewery bill.

Weak beer, known as small beer, was the staple drink for adults and children until safe drinking water became widely available, and tea became cheap enough for the general public to enjoy.

It was not unusual for the Butler (with the help of the Footman) to brew the beer themselves, from his own recipe; otherwise the big houses used an outside brewer to come in every three weeks for a day. Many of the estates used the same brewer.

RECIPES

Garlic Soup (Serves 6)

6 tablespoons whole garlic cloves
1 oz butter
4 tablespoon olive oil
35 fl oz chicken stock
3 egg yolks
Salt
Pinch cayenne and ground mace
6 rounds light bread (fresh)
2 tablespoons chopped parsley

Peel the garlic cloves carefully. Heat them in heavy pan in the butter with a tablespoon of olive oil. Cook gently over low heat for 15 minutes. Do not let the garlic brown. Pour on the stock and bring to boil for 20 minutes. Beat the egg yolks until they thicken and add the rest of oil, drop by drop. Stir in a few spoonful's of the soup into egg/oil mixture and add this new mixture <u>very slowly</u> to the pan, stirring constantly. Heat, but do not boil. Rub through a sieve into a warmed tureen. Season to taste. Add spices. Place a slice of fresh bread into a warm soup bowl and pour the soup over. Sprinkle with parsley, and serve.

Pea Soup (Serves 4–8)

1 lb dried peas (split)
2 oz diced salt pork or ham
6 oz chopped celery
6 oz chopped onion
70 fl oz cold water
1 ham bone
1 bay leaf
6 parsley stalks
10 whole allspice
1 blade mace
Salt and pepper
2 tablespoons chopped parsley

Soak dried peas in cold water overnight. Rinse and drain. Brown the pork or ham in a heavy pan, adding a little oil if the meat is very lean. Add the celery and onion and cook for 10 minutes. Add cold water, drained peas, ham bone, and the herbs and spices tied in a muslin. Simmer for 2 hours. Remove ham bone and muslin bag. Season to taste. Serve with parsley sprinkled on top and with fresh bread.

To Stew Carp

Place the carp in a large pan and cover in a mixture of vinegar, water, salt, a little horseradish, and lemon peel. Let them simmer gently until done enough.

For the sauce: Simmer gently the blood of carp, some good gravy, claret wine, a little horseradish, lemon peel, and 3 or 4 anchovies (the anchovies are first boiled whole until they are dissolved). Strain all through a sieve. Thicken it with butter and flour mixed together.

Optional additions: A few mushrooms or an oyster liquor.

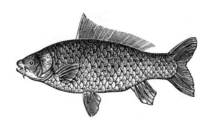

Soused Fish (Serves 4)
1 lb boiled or left-over fish
10 fl oz fish stock
10 fl oz vinegar
4 fennel leaves
3 bay leaves
2 cloves
12 peppercorns
3 slices lemon
Pinch of salt

Place pieces of fish in deep dish. Boil up fish stock with the vinegar while adding herbs, lemon and salt. Pour this over the fish and leave so the fish becomes saturated. Keep in a cold larder and serve with thin slices of brown bread.

Slipcoat Cheese (Special Recipe)
Take 3 quarts of new milk and a pint of cold water, one spoonful of rennet. Heat it up. Be sure not to break the curd, but lay it out whole. Let it stand for half an hour and lay a pound weight on it. Leave to stand for another hour, then turn it into a clean cloth and lay another pound weight on it. Let it stand for 2 hours then turn it and salt it. Let it stand another 2 hours longer. Take it out and keep it for 4 days. Afterwards put it into nettles or ashen leaves, shifting their position every day.

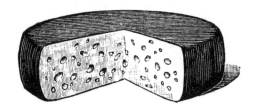

Spinach with Cream

Boil the spinach. Chop it very finely, squeeze it very dry,
then brown half a pound of butter. Stew it all together in
the butter. Add half a pint of cream and stew it together
again. Take it out, lay it smoothly in the serving dish and
stick little bits of fried bread all over it (like almonds in a
pudding).

Cinnamon Spinach

4½ lbs spinach
2oz butter
2½ tablespoons cream
Cinnamon
Salt
Sugar
Lemon rind

Trim and prepare spinach and wash well in cold water. Place in a pan with very little water, and salt to taste. Boil for 5–10 minutes till tender. Strain and press the spinach till free of water. Over a low heat, melt the butter in a heavy pan. Add cream, a pinch of sugar, salt and cinnamon to taste, plus a teaspoon of grated lemon rind. To this add the spinach and stir well. Serve at once.

Herb Omelette (Serves 2)

4 large eggs
Med onion
1 med boiled potato
1 clove garlic, chopped
Marjoram
Lovage
Chives } *1 teaspoon each, finely chopped*
Tarragon
Thyme
2 tomatoes
1½ tablespoons olive oil
Salt and pepper

Roughly chop onions, garlic, potatoes and tomatoes. Heat oil in heavy pan and gently fry the onions and garlic until soft. Add the tomatoes and potatoes and cook for 3–4 minutes. Break the eggs into separate bowl and beat them, adding herbs to taste and seasonings. Mix quickly with the vegetables in pan. Cook the underside if setting, then finish the omelette under a hot grill.

2-Tone Tomato Salad (4) – Sweet and Sour

6 tomatoes
1 med onion
Chives
Basil
Vinegar
2 tablespoons sugar
Water
Black pepper

Wash and dice the tomatoes and place in a bowl with finely chopped onions. Add a few sprigs of freshly chopped chives and a few torn basil leaves. Prepare the dressing by combining equal parts of vinegar and hot water with sugar. Pour this over the tomatoes, sprinkle very lightly with black pepper and keep cool. Serve cold.

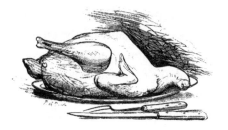

Blackened Seasonings – Good With Chicken or Fish

1 teaspoon sweet paprika

1 teaspoon cayenne pepper

2½ teaspoons salt

¾ teaspoon white pepper

1 teaspoon compressed onion

¾ teaspoon black pepper

1 teaspoon garlic

½ teaspoon dried thyme leaves

½ teaspoon dried oregano

DRINKS

Golden Cordial

Quart of brandy

Dram of cochineale

3 oz of stoned raisins

3 oz of comfits

Rind of an orange

2 sheets of leaf gold

Into the brandy, put the thin rind of an orange, the raisins, a dram of cochineale and the comfits. Close the jug with a stopper. Let it stand in a warm place for a week, shaking it often, then leave it standing for 2 days without shaking. Strain it off and add 2 sheets of leaf gold afterwards. (A dram of saffron may be added instead if preferred.)

Elderflower Cordial

20 elderflower heads
3 lbs sugar
2 pints boiling water
Juice of 2 lemons
Grated zest of 1 lemon
1 cinnamon stick (optional)

Place a layer of elderflowers in a clean bucket or large bowl. Cover them with some of the sugar. Repeat with more layers of elderflower and sugar until the bucket or bowl is ¾ full. Pour the boiling water over and add lemon juice and zest (can add the cinnamon stick here if wanted). Cover and leave overnight. Strain the liquid the next day and pour into sterilized bottles. This keeps for a few months.

MENUS

In eighteenth century, larger households often wrote their formal menus in French with sophisticated, trained cooks. The lady of the house would have spoken fluent French.

Lady Elizabeth's Menu from Lacock Abbey

Main Reference and Historical Sources

The author's private family collection of eighteenth-century domestic papers, designs, and account books, are from Lady Louisa Conolly (great-granddaughter of King Charles ll), who lived at Castletown, Ireland's first and finest Palladian country house. This collection is previously unpublished – and some is written in her own hand. Louisa was a lady of fashionable society and a friend of the fun-loving Duchess of Devonshire, who famously introduced her and her sisters to the 'High Hair' style of the day, with private tips on how to keep the hair 2–3 feet in the air.

Recipe and details are from: *The Children of Castletown House*, by Sarah Conolly-Carew, your author, published by The History Press.

The previously unpublished National Trust Collection of eighteenth-century recipes, remedies and garden planting from Lacock Abbey, Wiltshire, founded in 1229 by Ela, Countess of Salisbury, natural daughter-in-law of King Henry II. The abbey was converted into a country house by Sir William and Lady Sharington after the Dissolution of the Monasteries in the sixteenth century. In the eighteenth century, it was all the rage to collect and exchanged remedies, recipes, and tips from various distinguished patrons and guests and 'Lady Northumberland's remedies' are included here, as well as Lady Ivory's recipe to Sir John Talbot.

Papers and documents from Weddington Castle, by kind permission of weddingtoncastle.co.uk. The castle was originally owned by the 1st Duke of Suffolk, who was the father of Lady Jane Grey, the famous Nine-Day Queen. After Lady Jane Grey's execution for treason, the castle was forfeited to the Crown and later given by Queen Mary to the Earl of Huntingdon. The Weddington Castle Papers of the eighteenth and nineteenth centuries describe the duties of domestic servants both indoors and outdoors.

Familiar Wild Flowers, by F.E. Hume, published by Cassell & Co. Ltd, a division of Orion Publishing Group, with their kind permission.

Flowers of the Field, by Revd C.A. Johns FLS (1811–1874), published by SPCK Publishing, with their kind permission.

Household Notes

Household Notes

About the Author

Sarah Conolly-Carew Macpherson was born in Castletown House, Ireland's largest private home, a Neo-Palladian mansion on the banks of the River Liffey. She is the daughter of Lord and Lady Carew, and the grand-daughter of the 15th Earl of Lauderdale from Thirlestane Castle, Scotland. Sarah's ancestors include the sixteenth- and seventeenth-century Kings of England and Scotland, and the ancient Princes of Ireland. This book is based on a lifetime of memories of how best to live a very different kind of life. Sarah is the author of *The Children of Castletown House*, published in 2012 by The History Press.

About the Illustrator

Colour illustrations were painted by the late Mally Francis, Fellow of Linnean Society, Founder Chairman of Eden Project Florilegium Society, Fellow of Chelsea Physic Garden Florilegium Society, with exhibitions in London and Cornwall. These illustrations are paintings of the original plants and flowers from The Lost Gardens of Heligan, where Mally was Resident Artist, and where she gave Botanical Art Courses in the studio of her home. She died in 2019.